BORDERLANDS

Crossing Boundaries in Prayer

Dr Una Kroll is a priest in the Church in Wales, a medical doctor and a well-known author. Her most recent book, *Forgive and Live*, is published by Continuum. She lives in Monmouth.

BORDERLANDS

Crossing Boundaries in Prayer

Una Kroll

CANTERBURY PRESS

PRESS

Norwich

© Una Kroll 2000

Bible quotations are from the *New Revised Standard Version* of the Bible, © 1989 & 1995, the National Council of the Churches of Christ in the USA.

First published in 2000 by The Canterbury Press Norwich (a publishing imprint of Hymns Ancient & Modern Limited a registered charity) St Mary's Works, St Mary's Plain Norwich, Norfolk NR3 3BH

British Library Cataloguing in Publication Data

A catalogue record for this book is available from the British Library

ISBN 1–85311–361–1

Typeset by Rowland Phototypesetting Ltd, Bury St Edmunds, Suffolk Printed in Great Britain by St Edmundsbury Press Ltd, Bury St Edmunds, Suffolk

CONTENTS

BORDERLANDS
SERIES INTRODUCTION

'Borderlands are ambiguous places in which different cultures and traditions meet, frontiers from which the new can open up.' Esther de Waal, *A World Made Whole*.

The inspiration for this series of short books comes from the Society of the Sacred Cross, an Anglican contemplative community situated at Tymawr (Welsh for 'big house') Convent near Monmouth, South Wales. Its position on the border between England and Wales, and on the boundary between the Welsh and English provinces of the Anglican Communion, has made the Society more aware of its ability to provide a meeting ground for people of different religious backgrounds and varied experiences of God.

From this awareness has arisen a recognition that pilgrims on the Christian journey often enter border country. Political events, cultural changes and developments in science and technology are some of the stimuli that daily challenge us to apply a Christian mind to a fast-moving world. In our personal lives, an unexpected change can suddenly occur and we find ourselves in an unfamiliar landscape, unsure of which direction to take next.

Titles in this series are written out of the author's extensive experience in his or her field and are offered as companions and guides to the various personal, practical, spiritual or philosophical frontiers we may be exploring.

*

For further details about the Society of the Sacred Cross, please contact:

The Society of the Sacred Cross

Tymawr Convent

Lydart

Monmouth NR25 4RN

1

INTRODUCTION

Some time ago I came across a remarkable book about Helen Bamber, the founder of The Medical Foundation for the Care of Victims of Torture. In 1944, when she was twenty years old, Helen, a British Jew, volunteered to work for the Jewish Relief Unit in the British Zone of the occupied Germany. She was sent to Belsen where she worked with the survivors of the camp. Her encounter with the effects of prolonged suffering altered her life and she subsequently worked with victims of other regimes who had suffered torture. She also made connections between those who tortured other human beings and those who treated them without respect in institutions. This eventually led her to work with patients who had suffered from unethical medical experiments, and with children in hospital who suffered from the effects of separation from their parents.

At the end of the war Helen found herself disturbed by what she had seen and smelt at Belsen. She could not bring herself to enjoy hearing praise about the 'survival' of human beings who, in any case, should never have had to suffer the ghastly treatment meted out to them. Finding herself back in England, she decided to go and visit some men of the Northumberland Fusiliers who had been imprisoned by the Japanese after the fall of Singapore. This visit brought her to Berwick-upon-Tweed, a border town between the North of England and the Lowlands of Scotland.

Until the end of the fifteenth century Berwick was well acquainted with violence. It was a fought-over town, changing hands no less than eighteen times before the frontier between England and Scotland was finally settled. Later still, peace had come to the town. Legally it became a neutral zone between two countries until the latter half of the nineteenth century. By the twentieth century, however, Berwick-upon-Tweed had become a town where people on both sides of the border no longer needed to hate each other to the point of killing one another. It had become a place where people from different cultures were able to mingle in relative peace.

Helen Bamber's biographer, Neil Belton, writes of the effect of this border town on Helen in this way:

> Now[1] Berwick lies on a line between identities not worth killing for. Helen Bamber came to Berwick to find something in herself, as it is possible to do in border zones – there is a stillness, an absence of pressures, a sense of frontier isolation; as though the border were a real one, invisible but unforgotten. The usual rules don't seem to apply. Silence and survival and discretion have marked the place. Perhaps that is one of the reasons why it seemed so attractive to her when the world was insisting she remember.[2]

That paragraph about a border town between Scotland and England made me think about the town of Monmouth where I have lived for the past twelve years. Monmouth is close to the border between England and Wales. Like Berwick it has known violence in the past, but now it too lies 'on a line between identities not worth killing for'.

I came here as a widow in 1988 to live in close association with the nuns at Tymawr convent which is situated five miles outside the town.[3] Perhaps, unconsciously, I, like Helen, was attracted to border country, for my own life of prayer has been, and is, largely concerned with people who feel that their territories and identities *are* worth killing for.

This calling came to me as a young teenager when I was a medical student living in England during the Second World War, knowing that my three cousins, whom I loved dearly, were soldiers in the German army. During that war two of them were killed on the Russian front. The other was imprisoned for twelve years in a Soviet camp. Several years later I became a missionary doctor in Namibia at the time when the South West Africa People's Organisation (SWAPO) was beginning its guerrilla warfare against South Africa, the country that then administered the former German territory of South West Africa, or Namibia. Being torn between love and concern for people on both sides of a war gave me a desire to work for a just peace and reconciliation. That desire spread to other conflicts.

After our return to England in 1961 our family

was never again directly involved in war, but my work as a family doctor led me to work with people in conflict situations. From 1970, when I became a deaconess in the Church of England, I was caught up in the struggles of women in our country to gain equal opportunities for employment and equal pay for equal work. I also became personally involved in trying to persuade the Church of England to ordain women to the priesthood, a work which lasted until 1994 when the first women were admitted to that office in the Church. This work brought me into direct conflict with other Christians and it sometimes felt as if we were at war with each other, but it also reinforced my already present desire to work towards a just peace and reconciliation between people of strongly differing opinions.

By 1988, when I left the Church of England to become a deacon in the Church in Wales, I was experienced in the anatomy of conflict and familiar with its effects on one's life. What I have found through the experience of living in the border zone of Monmouth is the 'something in myself' that makes it possible to straddle the line between vigorous enemies, to cross borders, and even boundaries, in prayer so that Christ, present on both sides of an 'invisible but unforgotten' line, can reconcile enemies. After twelve years of living in this place of 'silence and survival and discretion', I know that it has given me gifts I could not have found elsewhere.

Such gifts make themselves known to their recipient gradually, almost unconsciously. At first, coming from a life of conflict in many different forms, the 'stillness, absence of pressures and frontier isolation' grate, induce guilt at being away from the front line, whatever its moral, social or political nature. Later, the terrible restlessness that comes from being in a place of peace when you have left others still fighting, (something that has afflicted every refugee I have met, everyone who has dropped out of a situation of intense conflict), gives way to new insights, new approaches to reconciliation, new courage, almost, I would say, to serenity. What I am describing is, of course, the experience of every Christian who follows Christ to the cross and discovers it to be the gateway to life. It is moving from human self-reliance to the strength given by grace. You start to learn that in the battle situations of life: you rediscover it through the disorientation of living in border country. If you live close to a boundary line for a length of time you eventually discover the humanity of people on both sides of a conflict. You also meet Christ on both sides of the frontier. Then it is that you can discover ways of living in reconciliation with God and with each other.

My experience of living in border country for a number of years has prompted me to reflect on its meaning for those of us who pray. In prayer we can cross boundaries fairly easily and discover the purpose of the space that lies on either side of an 'invisible, but unforgotten' boundary line. The word 'boundary' often implies demarcation between one country and another, between one county and another, between one home and another. Sometimes the boundary of a particular territory is marked out by gates and walls, moats and bridges, railings and fences. Sometimes it is quite invisible, denoted only on near-by road signs that tell you that you have moved from one country or territory to another. In prayer the boundaries are so ephemeral that one may forget they are there. Yet they are real. One should have respect for them and be aware of crossing them at all times. Respect and awareness are fairly easy to achieve in regard to place, but much less easy in regard to human beings whose individual spaces and boundaries are no less precious, but more invisible, sometimes less clearly defined, and sometimes less securely protected from unwanted invasion.

In this essay I am focusing on four areas of human experience where I think people whose chief work is prayer can, and sometimes should, cross boundaries. That is not to say there are not other equally important boundaries which are approached through border country, but these four have been and are important to me, which is why I want to explore them in some depth.

2

CROSSING BOUNDARIES
BETWEEN PLACE AND SPACE

When I was made a deacon in the Church in Wales in 1988 my vicar instructed me in my liturgical duties.

During the first Eucharist after ordination I was standing by the priest when he called on God the Father 'to sanctify with thy Holy Spirit these thy gifts of bread and wine, that we, receiving them according to thy Son our Saviour Jesus Christ's holy institution, may be partakers of his most precious Body and Blood'.[1] As he spoke these words the priest made the sign of the cross over the elements and spread his hands out in a gesture that suggested descent.

At that point in the service the chalice was covered with a pall, a piece of card covered in linen. I can remember thinking, 'Why not take it off so that the Holy Spirit can get through more easily?'

Simultaneously, I thought: 'But how absurd. If the risen Jesus could pass through a closed door (John 20:26) then the Holy Spirit won't have any difficulty with cardboard or linen!'

Needless to say this little episode showed me how literal my interpretation of the action of the Holy Spirit in the Eucharist was. Yet the very absurdity of my thoughts also led me to a greater truth about the Holy Spirit's tenderness towards us in that He never crosses boundaries, never forces entry, but asks for our co-operation in His coming, both in baptism and in the Eucharist.

The Holy Spirit who can transcend all boundaries, who can enter where and when He will, is gracious in waiting until He is invited to come and be present with us through baptism. The Holy Spirit is equally gracious in waiting to become present in the Eucharist so that the offered elements of bread and wine become for us the Body and Blood of Christ.

The simultaneous recognition that the Spirit can easily transcend any barriers, any boundaries, and that, paradoxically, the Spirit tarries upon human desire to make Christ incarnate in flesh, as He waited for the Virgin Mary's 'yes', has deeply affected the way

I tune in to His prayer in me. As in so many other people, that prayer often finds its expression in intercession for other people in other countries, other places, other times.

We know that the Holy Spirit intercedes for us 'with sighs too deep for words' (Rom. 8:26). All we have to do is to give ourselves to Him, to allow Him to pray in us, to listen to what He is doing and whispering. That gift of ourselves to God means that if He chooses to take us in prayer to Africa, for instance, or to Northern Ireland, or to a refugee camp, we are eager to go with Him. If He lays a burden of prayer upon us for a specific person, a family, a group of people or a whole community then we will readily take up that burden. This kind of 'tuning in' to the mind of Christ, as expressed by the indwelling Holy Spirit is quite difficult at a practical level because it involves us in being rooted in one place in our bodies and minds while at the same time we find ourselves elsewhere in the Spirit.

This ability to be in one place, one plane of experience, at the same time as being elsewhere in spirit is not always easy to handle, especially at the beginning of the life of prayer. Often people who pray in this way like to root themselves in silence, in a quiet space, in a church or chapel. With a still body, and uninterrupted opportunity, it is comparatively easy to be at that place and at the same time be elsewhere, in Kosovo, Venezuela, Chechnia, or any other place of disaster. It is far less easy to be in chapel singing a service of worship, or in an office typing a letter, and then suddenly find yourself in the middle of a war, or other disaster, in a distant country. Sometimes the difficulty is so great that it becomes noticeable to out-side observers: 'She's a dreamer', they might say of such a person, or, 'He's a bit absent minded.'

This difficulty can be overcome in a formal religious life by the careful use of time, and by judicious silence, which is a great help to this kind of 'double awareness', but the person who wants to live a life of prayer in the world is seldom able to control time or silence to any extent. He or she is invited to the stern discipline of 'double awareness' in the midst of considerable distraction and activity.

The easiest way to live comfortably with 'double awareness', is to develop a simple rhythm by which the body can act almost automatically at the same time that one's mind and heart are elsewhere. It is perfectly possible to make beds, wash up dishes, sweep floors, even do simple repetitive clerical work while interceding. It is impossible to pray in this way while driving a car, engaging in complex thought or conversation, or other intellectual exercises. This means that people who undertake continuous prayer as a way of life have to order their lives in tune with the Holy Spirit's prompting. If they set out to do that they will discover that the Holy Spirit acts within time and space but is not limited by either. An impulse to pray for a child being tortured in a far off country can be, and sometimes should be, incorporated into a present moment, but then if one is engaged in any activity that makes 'double awareness' inadvisable the Holy Spirit seems to be content to make that impulse dormant until it becomes possible to find more adequate time and space to deal with it. Moreover, if one finds oneself in such a predicament it is immensely helpful to be aware that one belongs to a praying body, the Church, in which at any given moment many other people may be free to intercede even if one is not able to do so oneself. In the divine economy the Holy Spirit inhabits their flesh and can use them for His purposes without in any way abandoning His use of one's own flesh in due course.

Contemplative living undoubtedly makes certain demands on those called to it. They *cannot* live frenetic lives of continuous activity without interruption. They *have* to order their lives to allow time for the Holy Spirit to engage their flesh in His work. Many of us called to this way of life know this instinctively. We set out with good intentions, but then find ourselves drawn into doing far too much. Attempts to do less may make us feel guilty when we cause others extra work. Moreover, any marked withdrawal from social engagement may lead to accusations of our being anti-social, or lazy, and compound our guilt. The remedy for these difficulties lies in adherence to a simple rule of life, recourse to a wise 'soul friend' and association with a religious community that knows and understands the necessity for rhythm in a life of prayer.

While it is apparent to anyone who undertakes prayer as a way of life that the Holy Spirit *can* transcend all kind of boundaries of place and space, I believe that the Holy Spirit is sometimes reluctant to cross boundaries. It seems to me that often He lingers in border country. In that border country pregnant with 'stillness, an absence of pressures, a sense of frontier isolation' there is time for the Holy Spirit, the indwelling Christ and the Father, to reveal His desire to us. There is time for us to discern how God's will towards this person, this family, this group, this community, even this country, fits into the pattern of God's purposes. Then we will find we also have time to conform our minds and hearts to God's will.

I can best describe this kind of involvement in the Holy Spirit's 'lingering' in border country by referring to my own experience of prolonged prayer for a friend who had cancer. My friend lived in another country, too far away for me to visit. She was a young middle-aged Christian who had experienced great unhappiness in her personal life. Just as everything seemed to be sorting itself out for her she developed cancer. She rang me up to ask for prayers for a forthcoming operation. Her disease was in its early stages and her prognosis was good.

I settled down to pray. I found myself in a place of bewildering uncertainty. I wanted to pray for her recovery, but I could not hear the Holy Spirit guiding my prayer in this way. I think that even then I probably knew God's ultimate desire for my friend, but

I could not face the possibility of her death. I was simply not ready. So I prayed with all my heart for my distant friend's recovery. At that point I had a great desire to persuade the Holy Spirit to pray in the same direction. Over the succeeding months I never got the answer I wanted so much to hear. I think now that both my friend and I needed time in that 'border' country to be able to come to terms with our impending separation, and that God in His graciousness gave it to us.

My friend made a good initial recovery from the operation and for the next year all appeared to be going well for her. Then one day I had the dreaded phone call: 'It's back', she said, 'God can do anything. Pray for me.' 'I will,' I promised her, but at that moment the Holy Spirit beckoned me across the boundary and I knew I must begin to pray for her release into the healing of death. I cancelled some engagements and increased my time of prayer so that I could be with God and her in the waiting. There was time to allow the Holy Spirit to take us both across the boundary between life and death so that I could see how I could best help her as she made the crossing. I was also able to glimpse how our relationship would continue when she was with the communion of saints in heaven.

My friend died peacefully a few weeks later. She had the time she needed to mend a broken relationship. There was time to give thanks for that reconciliation. I had time to be grateful for her life and to mourn her passing.

It is not at all easy to intercede in this way. So often we convince ourselves that God wants what we want. We think of all the reasons, and there are many, why God should spare this person whose life is so evidently useful and whom we love so much. God knows that we are human: we need to argue our case, we need to try and persuade God to do what we want. It is not at all surprising that we sometimes find it very difficult to accept that we may be wrong. Indeed, I think that this kind of arguing with God, even at times raging at God, is all part of our intercession, a healthy way of communicating with God. Yet, in the end, if we keep an open mind and listen intently, we can sometimes see the whole situation from God's perspective, and begin to understand. Nevertheless, there have been many times in my life when I have not understood, have not accepted the rightness of what is happening. All I have been able to do is to grit my teeth and say with Job: 'Though he slay me, yet will I trust in him: but I will maintain mine own ways before him' (Job 13:15).

Intercessory prayer is a privileged part of every Christian's life. It is, I think, important not to be intrusive. As I get older I do not often say, as I once did, with a light heart, 'I will pray for you', nor these days do I make lists and go through them every day. Instead, I usually wait to be asked, sometimes by the person concerned, often by the Holy Spirit who brings someone to mind quite spontaneously and perhaps unexpectedly. I read the newspapers, watch television news and I wait until I am drawn into prayer for a particular person, family, group or community. When the Holy Spirit does prompt me to prayer I know it will demand time, energy and commitment so that I can listen to His prayer in me and become aware of His taking that concern to Jesus who stands ever before God making intercession for us.

Yes, it is good to be aware of borders and boundaries. In the interior life there are no huge walls and barriers that prevent the Holy Spirit from going anywhere, but there are transition points like stiles between two fields or the sea edge where land and sea meet. We do well sometimes to pause awhile before moving from one kind of terrain to another, from one experience to another to consider its implications as well as its possible consequences. This is particularly important in regard to the borders and boundaries between people on opposite sides of any conflict, as I shall hope to show in the next chapter.

3

CROSSING BOUNDARIES BETWEEN LIKENESS AND DIFFERENCE

Some years ago I went to speak at a large meeting that had been convened to discuss the ordination of women in the Church of England. My own view – that it was not only possible but desirable to ordain women to the Anglican priesthood, for the sake of the mission of the Church in the twentieth century – was unpopular at the time. My opponent in the debate was a well-known, and much-loved, woman worker in the local church. As I walked into the room I could sense the hostility that greeted me. Ignoring it as best I could, I opened the discussions with a quiet logical approach. The other speaker then rose and developed the opposing point of view in an attractive way. I listened carefully. Her proposition, largely derived from her understanding of the Old Testament, was that women could, and should, be prophets, but not priests. I had not heard that particular argument before, and it interested me greatly.

Her line of reasoning was that priests are guardians of continuity. They tend to perpetuate the tradition of their cult or church by maintaining doctrines and enshrining them in their rites. Prophets declare the truth that God tells them to proclaim. Consequently they often challenge the established roles and customs of their time. Some people think it is impossible to speak out against the errors of one's time and still belong to a professional body that exists to maintain the established order.

As I listened I countered some of the logic from personal experience. I had met professional priests who had acted prophetically. They had pointed out the reforms that were needed and had worked for necessary change. When they became active reformers these prophetic priests had often upset the majority of their fellow clergy and sometimes they had disturbed the whole Church. I knew the value of prophecy coming from within the ranks of the clergy, but I also knew how difficult that role was. So there was more than a small spark of sympathy in me when I heard the arguments advanced by my colleague.

During the ensuing discussions I was not surprised to find myself in a minority. I *was* surprised by my own ability to get into the opposing side's shoes. Indeed, I was quite unnerved. The hostility to my approach remained evident. It was as if a barrier had been erected that prevented many people present from being able to meet me in open discussion. I, however, had crossed an invisible boundary. I had 'gone over', or, rather, 'crawled under' the hostility to find empathy with my opponent.

The debate ended, as expected, with a large vote against my proposition. I was left to struggle with the change in me. Before this discussion I had been a protagonist for women's ordination, someone who could only see one point of view. After it, I had become a person who could empathize with a different point of view, although I still thought that the Anglican Church should welcome women into its ordained ministries. I also saw the need for reconciliation between people who were deeply opposed to each other. My calling to pray for, and work for reconciliation among Christians in the Anglican

Church was recognized during that evening and it remains with me still.

There is an interesting end to this story. My principal opponent at that debate became a priest several years before I did. Experience in the limitations on her work as a deaconess convinced her, as it did so many others, that she could exercise a more effective ministry were she to be a priest, and when the Church of England came round to that view as well she went forward happily. The Church in Wales did not decide to ordain women until three years later. I, left to struggle with a dual vocation of prophet and priest, have always been grateful for the change in me that took place during that discussion.

I have witnessed many conflicts during my professional life as a doctor who subsequently became a priest of the Church in Wales. Most of these conflicts have involved me as someone who tried to mediate between two people in disagreement. It is that experience that I now offer for reflection. Most of us feel comfortable with people whose views agree with our own. Many of us can tolerate disagreements with those whom we love. Constructive controversy can enrich us and expand our horizons. When, however, dissension is so serious that it affects our freedom to live in a particular way, we may fall out with each other or even go to war with each other.

Human beings who cannot agree, who cannot find their way through serious disagreements, settle their disputes in a number of different ways. The most obvious way is to separate. Children leave home, sometimes never to return. Husbands and wives divorce. Politicians resign on grounds of conscience. Priests opposed to the ordination of women leave their church for another that does not permit women to be ordained. Separation is effective, but it carries with it profound disappointment, a sense of permanent loss of relationship, sometimes even a feeling of bitterness that one has been 'forced out' when one did not want to leave.

Another outcome of serious disagreement is to go to law to resolve an apparently insoluble problem. Many people solve disputes that arise out of property and boundary problems by going to an independent mediator, a judge versed in law, a person who is not involved but who can be trusted to form an independent and just opinion. Hence people in dispute about the ownership of their boundary hedges, or about neighbours' parking rights, can sometimes settle those disputes in court. Again, there is sometimes a lingering feeling of injustice if the case is not settled according to one's advantage.

Some people, particularly those in power, decide to go to war to settle territorial disputes. Countries with territorial claims will sometimes invade a neighbouring country in the hope of gaining ground, but they will also generally know that after a suitable time, and much loss of life, they will have to consult the United Nations. They will have to come to the conference table to secure peace.

A more terrible solution to disputes, disagreements and territorial wars comes through a desire to eliminate one's opponents through murder, genocide or forced exile. This aggressive approach seems increasingly common at the beginning of the twenty-first century and is symptomatic of a human race that has lost its understanding of God and of itself. Such descent into degraded aggression against one's own kind is a sign of despair in one's own capacity for becoming truly human.

Christians who pray cannot whole-heartedly agree with any of these solutions, simply because they know that God has created them to live in unity with each other within the love of their Creator. They may have to accept separation, recourse to law, even war, as the only way of looking for a solution to an apparently insoluble problem, but they will not want to look for that kind of resolution from the outset. They will pursue visible reconciliation for as long as they can. Ultimately, even if they fail outwardly, they will believe that reconciliation can, and does, take place through Christ.

My principal concern in this chapter is to show how those who pray can accompany people on both sides of any dispute. It is something to which I am well accustomed since at an early age my mother and father parted company, much to my distress, and I spent much time then, and as a young adult, praying for their reconciliation. It came in a wholly unexpected way when my mother was dying. As I have already said, in my late teen-age years I found myself living in England during the Second World War knowing that my relatives and friends were killing, and being killed by relatives and friends on the other side.[1] As a Christian adult I have spent the majority of my working life with people who want to be reconciled to each other at some level of experience.

One prerequisite to this kind of prayer for reconciliation is an ability to cross the boundaries that divide people, to stand with both sides in empathy. One may do that by sitting on the fence and refusing to take sides. That is the way often adopted by professional negotiators, mediators and judges. There is an advantage in such neutrality and from a practical point of view this way works well. If one is called to prayer, however, I feel that another way is possible.

In this second way of being with people in dispute the one who is called to the prayer of reconciliation does not necessarily start from a neutral position. He or she may, for instance, be opposed to the use of nuclear weapons, may even work publicly for their abolition. Such people have their feet planted firmly on one side of the boundary dividing them from those of a different view. Yet, in prayer, prayer that is united with Christ who stretches His arms across boundaries in love for all, those who pray for reconciliation in this way are sensitive enough to be able to understand, sympathize.

It is sometimes argued that such a stance could be

partisan and prejudiced from the outset. A judge of the British Court of Appeal who did not disclose that he was a member of Amnesty International was, for instance, thought to be compromised and unable to sit in judgement on a former South American president who was accused of war crimes.[2] Consequently there had to be a rehearing of the extradition proceedings. There is, however, a difference between having to sit in judgement on someone and praying for all the disputants in any conflict. What one cannot do in a public court of law is sometimes possible, even effective, in prayer where all judgement is suspended and one's sole object is to help people in conflict to meet Christ in one another and each other in Christ.

In one small Christian community of my acquaintance, for instance, a group of people with different views came together to pray with each other before the final debate in 1992 on the ordination of women to the priesthood of the Church of England. They did not come to pray against each other. They did not attempt to change each other's minds. They simply wanted to find each other in God. And did. After the debate was concluded and women were ordained to the priesthood of the Church of England some members of that group left the church of their birth and became members of other churches. Some stayed and tried to live with their differences. All remained in charity with one another.

The discovery that one's opponents are as human as oneself, as intelligent, as sincere, as Christian, is a tremendous blessing. It enables differences to be held and maintained without rancour. It makes it possible to handle continued disagreement sensitively. It allows one to be sorrowful that one can no longer enjoy full communion with each other while at the same time meeting one another in the 'kiss of peace' that coming into Christ's presence together bestows on all who dare to meet in this way.

This kind of prayer work is demanding. If people called to pray in such a way venture across the border they may well find themselves absorbing so much of the other side's point of view that they find themselves plunged into doubts about their own beliefs. In the end doubt, rightly used, increases conviction, but it sometimes feels as if one is in the middle of a tornado clinging on to a thin branch of a tree that looks as if it is going to be uprooted at any minute. The only remedy for this kind of experience is to let go of the branch and tree of conflicting opinions and run instead to hide in the cleft of the Rock, Christ Himself.

Such work also needs stamina. Those who pray for reconciliation in this way may find themselves growing weary of the torrents of hatred and abuse that are still being hurled at the people on the other side of the boundary long after a dispute has been ended by a decision, be it a decision to leave home, or seek a divorce, or resign from a committee, or be it a decision made by a synod or governing body of a church. Again, there is only one remedy, Christ who invites those who are 'weary and heavy laden' (Matt. 11:28)[3] to seek refuge in Him.

There is another consequence of being called to become an 'ambassador for reconciliation' (2 Cor. 5:20). Those who say, 'yes' and undertake this work will have to look at the pain and wounds of all the disputants. They may have to watch people becoming bitter, full of desire for revenge, hardly left with any love. They may be called upon to bandage the wounds of their own enemies. They may have to exercise selfless love in the attempt to bring people together in Christ through, and in, prayer. No one can do this kind of work in his or her own strength. People called to the prayer of reconciliation know that they can only go where they are called because Christ accompanies them.

All this is true, but, as someone who knows she is called to such work, I know that the joy of watching Christ effect this work of reconciliation is greater than any difficulty that comes from being the 'go-between', 'go across the boundaries' person whom Christ uses in this kind of incarnate work by His Body, the Church. I thank God every day for what I see being done by the Blessed Trinity on earth.

4

CROSSING BOUNDARIES
BETWEEN GOOD AND EVIL

In 1932 a young woman called Iulia de Beausobre was imprisoned by the Soviet authorities on charges of subversive behaviour. She was put into solitary confinement.

Now solitude of any kind forces one to confront both good and evil within oneself. That is why it can be such a powerful weapon in the hands of those who want to subdue a person and bring them to heel. Although Iulia knew this and had armed herself, as so many political prisoners do, with memorized portions of well-loved, well-read books, recallable images of former happy times, and a disciplined routine to cope with her confinement to a small space, she was still vulnerable to her interior 'demons' and she knew it.

Iulia's book about her experiences in prison, *The Woman Who Could Not Die,*[1] reveals the way in which she was confronted by internal accusations about her moral failures. Left alone in a silent cell, exposed to the glare of perpetual light from a naked bulb hung from the ceiling on a length of bare flex, Iulia saw herself as being 'a repulsive imbecile and a revolting moral coward'.[2] She worried about the fate of her husband who had been arrested the week before her own detention. (She did not know until some time after her release that he had been shot.) She dreaded her forthcoming interrogation. She felt a profound lack of moral fibre within herself.

It was when she was in this state of terror that a sense of peace came to her from outside herself, a peace that filled her and also radiated out from her as she was escorted to her interrogation. She clung to that peace throughout the eight months that she remained in Lubyanka prison, throughout successive interrogations. It was her repeated experience of mental torture, inflicted on her by her interrogators, that helped her to see that she could, if she chose, collude with the external evil by reinforcing it by her own weakness, cowardice, imbalance, lack of serenity and hatred for those who were submitting her to such cruelty.[3] At one stage, months into her captivity, as she hung between the good in the depths of herself and the evil that is in all of us, she chose to cross the boundary between the good and evil in herself and move towards love, love that extended even to those who were hurting her.

Iulia did not come to this heroic decision without confronting her own faults and sins, without recognizing in her self her own capacity for hatred and cruelty. In a subsequent booklet, *Creative Suffering*,[4] written years after her release from captivity, she comments that it is possible to participate in an event of torture either as the victim or the torturer. As a victim, the one being destroyed by external evil, it is relatively easy to identify with the person of Christ, to see his redemptive acts from within your own crucifixion. As the torturer, bound into sadistic cruelty by the knowledge of one's own capacity for cruelty, you are inviting 'the onslaught of terrible lusts, the lust for power, and what in its lesser degree, is lightly termed bullying'.[5] From both stances, Iulia says, 'you can gain insight into God's composition for the deed'.[6] What she means by this phrase is, I think, that if you meditate on all the characters in the crucifixion of Christ, and if you clearly see the event both from His perspective and also from that of those who were intent on killing Him, and who saw Christ from that angle, you can see that God's ultimate 'composition for the deed' is the eventual salvation of human kind.[7]

Iulia de Beausobre was a remarkable woman. Her outward suffering made it possible for her to describe the experience of the intimacy of good and evil in human beings. She saw that each human being contains the potential to become a good person who may become the victim of torture. All human beings, nevertheless, also have a shadow side, a propensity for evil that may permit them to become torturers. Iulia, herself a tortured victim, recognized her own capacity for evil, and she also saw that her oppressors had a potential for good within them.

Many of us do not have Iulia's keen awareness of the companionship, yet distinction, of good and evil within human personalities. We can sense there *is* a boundary between good and evil, but we cannot easily define where that boundary is, nor, since the angels of darkness are so adept at mimicking the angels of light, can we always distinguish between good and evil impulses in ourselves. Indeed, in one sense there is polarity of good and evil rather than separation between them, but in another sense it is important at a practical level to be able to see them as entities held together in God's purpose, but sufficiently distinct to offer us an opportunity to choose between life and death (Deut. 30:19).

Iulia de Beausobre developed her profound insights into the mystery of the interface between good and evil through the experience of external evil resonating with her own interior chaos. Other Christians, who do not have to encounter what she did, but who are called to live lives of prayer, may come to a place where they too become aware of what it means to cross the boundary between good and evil. Those who do this may 'become fully aware of the real place of the event in God's composition'(God's ultimate purposes). They may reach this awareness from the side of the victim of evil or from the side of the perpetrator of an evil deed.[8]

It is in prayer that some Christians find they are called to experience the onslaughts of evil, indeed, at times they may feel almost consumed by it. A devout

Christian woman may attend a Eucharist and find herself overwhelmed by a spirit of blasphemy. A man, normally regarded as a 'holy' man, engaged in a struggle for racial justice may find himself hating racial supremacists to the point where he is willing to kill some of them. A Christian, pulled by the Holy Spirit into an area where genocide is taking place, may feel so embittered that it seems impossible to believe in God.

When people first find themselves engaged in this kind of prayer they may feel intimidated by the strong feelings that burst into their consciousness. They do not know where those feelings are coming from. Some undoubtedly come from within themselves; sometimes they are the product of long-repressed emotions. But that is not the whole story. Some of these negative thoughts and feelings come by absorption of the collective emotional energies that are being generated in any other place where blasphemies, strong antipathies and destructive actions are actually taking place. Since particle-wave energies, such as light and radio waves, can travel great distances it should not surprise us to find that emotional vibrations can be, and sometimes are, communicated over long distances. People who are sensitive can tune into these vibrations and interpret them in much the same way that a radio or television receiver can analyse and transmit waves into audible sound or pictures. Some negativity may not come from human beings at all. It may emanate from collective energies of spiritual evil, the entities that St Paul described when he said: 'For we wrestle not against flesh and blood, but against principalities, against powers, against the rulers of the darkness of this world, against spiritual wickedness in high places' (Eph. 6:12). Those who find themselves experiencing these powerful negative feelings during prayer in this way may feel frightened, or disgusted, or even despairing. That is natural at first, but we need to learn how to abide in evil without becoming evil, how to look towards God in hope. It is not that one will often see God in this situation. All one can hope for is to see God's 'composition for the deed'. Even that is very difficult until after one has emerged from the immediate experience.

There are some practical ways of assisting God if one finds oneself in such a state. The first is to keep calm, to avoid struggling against the negativity. Skirmish only increases the tension. If, instead, one can regard the negative feelings as an 'offering' and bring them to Christ in humility they can be absorbed into his love. This steady quiet presentation to the Source of all healing may have to continue for some time, but with patience one finds that the negativity is absorbed and one returns to peace. It is unpleasant to come to Holy Communion, for instance, filled with blasphemy and hatred for Christ, but such feelings are no reason to keep away. Indeed, it is all the more important to approach Love for He alone can reconcile us, indeed all that is hostile to Himself, to God.

The second is to learn to live by the tenets that spring from theology rather than paying attention to feelings. People who pray in this way are not safe unless they adhere to the good doctrine of their own salvation through Christ's atoning love on the cross. It is also helpful if they know certain biblical passages sufficiently well to be able to call on them in such times of crisis. If, for instance, one finds oneself engulfed in hatred for a particular person who is one's close neighbour in church, it is a great help to be able to counter one's powerful feelings with words of scripture, such as, 'Love your enemies and pray for those who persecute you' (Matt. 5:44), or, 'Those who are well have no need of a physician, but those who are sick. Go and learn what this means, "I desire mercy, not sacrifice". For I have come to call not the righteous but sinners' (Matt. 9:12–13). Knowing oneself to be sick and in need of a physician helps one to go forward to receive grace, rather than refraining from Holy Communion in the mistaken belief that one is unworthy to receive. Above all, I think, it is necessary to remember that one is a baptized Christian, a child of God, an inheritor of the kingdom. Reliance on Christ's redeeming love, not on one's own feelings, is the way by which even the strongest negativity can be overcome.

These observations come from experience with people who are appalled by their hostile emotions. Often they are so upset by them that they feel they have committed an unforgivable sin, that they are damned, or that they need to be exorcized. In fact all they need to do is to learn about the polarity between good and evil, namely that whenever they are experiencing strongly negative feelings they can be assured that there *are* positive forces within them, even though they are not aware of them, which will contain and absorb those feelings. At such times they need to live by the theological belief that nothing, nothing at all, 'neither death, nor life, nor angels, nor rulers, nor things present, nor things to come, nor powers, nor height, nor depth, nor anything else in all creation, will be able to separate us from the love of God in Christ Jesus our Lord' (Rom. 8: 38–39).

All that is true, but it is *not* easy to put into practice. It needs years of patience to be able to live theologically rather than experientially. It is helpful to know this. It is even more helpful if one can find a wise 'soul friend' who can help one to remain steady under assaults of all kinds, whether those assaults come from within one's own personality or from outside one's self. Eventually, I believe, many people who make prayer central to their lives, both those who live in community and those who live their lives of prayer in a more solitary way, find their way through to a 'double vision' in which they can simultaneously perceive good and evil as part of God's 'composition of the deed', God's ultimate purpose for humankind and for each individual. This 'double vision' is an extension of the 'double awareness' referred to in the first chapter. Whereas 'double awareness' refers to the ability to be in two places at one and the same time, 'double vision' refers to the ability to see God's purpose from the depths of good and evil at the same time.

Sin and suffering lose their ability to shock. Evil is seen to be a temporary phenomenon, permitted by God and fulfilling God's purpose in that it can provoke godliness and righteous living. The Deuteronomic boundary between good and evil is still there and continual choices between the two still have to be made, but crossing the boundary from good to evil in prayer no longer has the capacity to induce fear and disgust. It is the way to reconciliation and eternal life.

5

CROSSING BOUNDARIES
BETWEEN LIFE AND DEATH

Pilgrims who go to Iona or to Bardsey Island off the Lleyn peninsula in North Wales often say that these islands are 'thin' places, places where the veil between heaven and earth seems to be almost non-existent. It is probably significant that both these islands are the burial grounds of hundreds of saints who have given their lives to prayer. The memory traces they have left behind them, together with the theological reality of the communion of saints, that unites living and dead, produces a tangible communication between the living and the dead.

One does not have to go to a holy place to experience this unity of living and dead. It is present every time a Eucharist is celebrated. It is present in prayer. It is manifest in some people. The Eucharist, as we know it on earth, takes place in half an hour, or about an hour if the rite is sung and there is a sermon. The rite, whether it be celebrated in a Roman Catholic, Orthodox, Anglican or Non-conformist church, contains words that were once used by Jesus at the Last Supper. Bread, the ordinary stuff of life, is taken, blessed, broken and shared among the assembly. Wine, fruit of the vine, is taken, poured out, blessed, and shared. In performing those simple actions the Church recalls Christ's taking of our human flesh, the blessing of his earthly ministry, the breaking of his life upon the cross, the renewed blessing of his resurrected and ascended life and the sharing of it with his people through the coming of the Holy Spirit at Pentecost. There is, throughout the rite, a joining of heaven and earth. Those on earth are lifted up into heaven where the Eucharist, the perpetual exchange of love between Father, Son and Holy Spirit, is always taking place, the mysterious interaction between life and death, joy and suffering, love and hate, continues 'world without end'.

Many people who attend a Eucharist find it difficult to remain focused on its action. They get distracted by music, other people's fidgets, children's noises, their interior feelings, their neighbour's needs. Even quite little things like the priest's clothes, or his demeanour can prevent people from being able to cross the boundary between heaven and earth during a Eucharist. They remain earthbound. They sometimes get so distracted by small irritations that they cannot see anything else. Going to church may even become a negative experience. People may even withdraw from congregational worship for such reasons, but even if they do continue to attend they may miss out on the transcendent mystery of the Eucharist and see it as a communal meal, a feast of love, a feast shared with those who are present.

By way of contrast there are those who lose themselves wholly in the mystery. They are lifted up to heaven in communion with God but have real difficulty in relating to their neighbour, for instance, through the kiss of peace. They have real problems in tolerating the human failings of priest and people. They may even find it hard to accept that the Body and Blood are as precious to their earth-bound neighbour as to themselves. They remain 'head in the sky' and cannot find ways of 'coming down to earth' again. Such people may find the presence of children, or communion in the round, difficult to tolerate. By nature many of them prefer to worship at a quiet Eucharist in the early morning or in the serene and measured ritual of a convent chapel.

At times all of us will find ourselves earthbound or caught up into 'the third heaven'. Yet the gifts we can receive in the Eucharist are poured out in their fullest measure if we can move easily between heaven and earth, if we can live in the border country of approach, if we can move comfortably towards the boundary that seems to separate them, as it separates earth and sea. That boundary is a meeting place, a place of intersection, a place of grace.

It is not the purpose of this chapter to make liturgical suggestions as to how transcendence and immanence can be held together in the Eucharist; rather it is to see how living with the Eucharist as the central theme of our life can enhance the way in which we can hold heaven and earth, transcendence and immanence, together in our ordinary lives and bring the gift of border living into every aspect of our experience.

Central to every Eucharist, central to every created life, is the fact of death. Christ's death on the cross is at the heart of every Eucharist. So is it in all life. Human beings, creatures who are consciously self-aware, know that from the moment we are born we carry in our bodies the seeds of death. During our earthly existence we gradually come to terms with death. Some people, especially those who are young and active and, as they think, far distant from its actuality in their own lives, can ignore the fact of death for a long time. Others are confronted with it early in life through the death of close relatives, young friends or well-loved animals.

Death is a shock to all of us. We can be touched by it intimately, yet somehow avoid thinking of ourselves as mortal. Human beings 'cannot bear very much reality,' T. S. Eliot wrote,[1] and many of us are adept at avoiding the fact of our own death until we come close to it ourselves. Christians, however, are constantly in touch with death through their intimacy with Christ in the Eucharist, through their meditations on Scripture and through prayer. So they have more opportunity than most people to see death as a gateway to resurrection life. They have the chance to see the border country between life and death as a gift to be used to the full. They can learn to live in border country without being afraid, seeing it as 'a place of stillness, absence of pressures and frontier isolation'.[2]

The people who have helped me personally to appreciate the border country between life and death, between heaven and earth, between the cross and resurrection that is at the heart of the Eucharist, are the people who have learnt to live close to the boundary this side of death, or who are learning to live in that way.

When my husband and I knew that his time on earth was limited by encroaching disease in which destructive forces were stronger than his bodily life force, we found ourselves living in that border country this side of death, in what we came to think of as 'end time'. We knew that Leo was going to die fairly soon, but we did not know when, or exactly how. We began to live each day in a new way. Initially, while he was still fairly well, we took pleasure in the quality of each present moment. We determined to live each day as if there was another to come, while being aware that another might not dawn. So we found ourselves in a place where delight was heightened. We gained intense pleasure from seeing a garden flower in bloom. Next year only one of us would see it. Meantime it was an intensely shared experience. If I wanted to buy him a present I no longer waited until his birthday. I bought it the day I saw it. Every day became a potential birthday. If Leo wanted to go for a drive to see some of the countryside he loved so much, we went that very day. If he wanted wine I bought it, even if it was a day on which we would not normally drink wine.

Later on, when such pleasures were limited by physical weakness, they were replaced by words of love and tenderness and thankfulness. We were grateful to have that time to speak to each other of our gratitude for one another. Many people do not get that gift.

Our heightened awareness was not all pleasurable, of course. I, in particular, was aware that my heightened perception of pain, his pain and mine at parting, was increasing my sensitivity to all pain, all suffering, all parting. Watching the news each day was part of our living in 'end time', part of my own daily intercession, but as Leo moved inexorably into the place where there is an absence of pressure, an absence of engagement in the world's affairs because of one's approaching death, I was left still engaged while he moved on to a new place. Watching the news without him, seeing the tortured, those emaciated by hunger, the dying, the prisoners awaiting execution, moved me to tears. My tears for others in his kind of situation were painful but also healing.

As we approached the frontier of separation, where the part of his journey that Leo must make on his own began, the border I could not cross with him, except in spirit, we met it with shared silence. It was the kind of silence that sometimes descends on people who are at worship together, a silence too deep for words, a silence of awe. At the moment of his death I broke that silence, wanting to say one last word of love, and my wise doctor son put his finger to his lips and urged me to refrain, lest my voice should hold his father back from crossing the boundary. I have always been grateful to him for that wisdom.

After Leo's death, I discovered that I knew how to live in 'end time', how to make use of stillness, the absence of pressures that comes to people who are free from the ambitions and preoccupations of their younger years and are able to live in the present moment with joy. I began to know a little about the sense of isolation that must come to all who begin to live in the border country between life and death by reason of bereavement, serious illness, age and increasing bodily diminishment.

My own experience is by no means rare. I have met many people who have been able to live in 'end time' in this way though fewer who connect the way they are living to the Eucharist. For me, however, the connection between experience and the Eucharist is clearest in regard to my relationship to those whom I knew and loved in life, but who are now dead.

Grief in bereavement is natural and it sometimes means that we on our side of the border feel cut off from those on the other side, that we cannot sense their 'living presence' in eternity. That happened to me, but by faith I believe that the communion of saints, the living and dead members of the household of God, is a reality and I know that when I come to the altar rail to receive Holy Communion all barriers between ourselves and the dead are removed by our mutual sharing of Christ's life. That reality is precious to me.

The actions of the Eucharist can be re-enacted

every day in ordinary life. Each day we take from the earth, from the fruits of other people's labours, from those whom we meet, or for whom we pray in silence, from the living and the dead. Every day we can give thanks for what we receive from God's hand, either directly through prayer and reading, or from other people. We can always break some of what we have received in order to share it with others, either through our lives of prayer or in our service to God's created world and its inhabitants. If we think about the four actions of Christ at the Last Supper – taking, blessing, breaking and sharing – and if we carry them out every day, then we shall enter the mystery of his own life, passion, death and resurrection, we shall enter the border country between life and death and be ready to cross over the boundary between them to eternal life without anxiety.

This kind of 'tuning in' to the Eucharist, this kind of Eucharistic living, is a great strength when one becomes ill, even when young, or reaches an age where one can no longer get to church to worship with other Christians. Many ill or older people are physically 'cut off' from their Christian community but if we find a way each day of living at the heart of the Eucharist we know that we are never isolated. We are able to cross the boundaries of space and place to be with our fellow Christians wherever they are. We are able to cross boundaries of difference and find our unity with others. We are able to use the polarity of good and evil in intercessory prayer and we are able to commune with the dead in a way that people more active than ourselves cannot do so easily.

Our communion with each other is emphasized for me by words of St Paul which reinforce my perception of reality:

> We do not live to ourselves, and we do not die to ourselves. If we live, we live to the Lord, and if we die, we die to the Lord; so then, whether we live or whether we die, we are the Lord's. For to this end Christ died and lived again, so that he might be Lord of both the dead and the living. (Rom. 14:7–9)

Life from its beginning to its end is an adventure. It offers challenges that need to be met. It invites growth. It is rich in suffering but also in joy. It has been a privilege to spend the last years of my own life in border country, a place marked by silence and survival and discretion. These years began at Tymawr and the discoveries made there have enriched the subsequent years lived in a small house in the churchyard of a parish church. Here silence is deep and welcoming. The house bears evidence of its own survival through careful renewal of its fabric, and discretion is its watchword since so many secrets are enfolded in its walls. Within its shelter many boundaries have been crossed, not only by myself but also by my predecessors. We dwell in communion with each other across the boundaries of space and time. The former inhabitants of this place make their own distinctive contribution to the life of present and future occupants, but they do not constrict growth and they positively invite those who are living now to cross new boundaries wherever they are to be found.

May such work continue in many places. And may many more places become 'thin' places where the veil is lifted, the boundaries dissolve and God's glory shines forth in all its splendour.